QUOTABLE
HOGAN

QUOTABLE
HOGAN

*Words of Wisdom, Success, and Perseverance
by and about* **BEN HOGAN,**
Golf's Ultimate Perfectionist

Rich Skyzinski

TowleHouse Publishing
Nashville, Tennessee

TowleHouse books are distributed by National Book Network (NBN), 4720 Boston Way, Lanham, Maryland 20706.

Library of Congress Cataloging-in-Publication data is available.
ISBN: 1-931249-07-5

Cover design by Gore Studio, Inc.
Page design by Mike Towle

Printed in the United States of America
1 2 3 4 5 6 — 05 04 03 02 01

Contents

Acknowledgments

I WISH TO THANK several people for their invaluable coopera-
tion and assistance with this book: Maxine Vigliotta, Tanya
Gray, Marty Parkes, Rand Jerris, and Patty Moran at the United
States Golf Association; Jimmy Burch at the *Fort Worth Star-
Telegram*; Tammy Fabrizio and Stacy Benvenuto in the
Programming Department at ESPN; the Special Collections
Division of the library at the University of Texas-Arlington; the
Special Collections Division at the Dallas Public Library; Hogan
biographer and author Curt Sampson; and former *Cleveland Plain
Dealer* sportswriter Bill Livingston. My wife, Susan, deserves the
greatest thanks for her inconceivably wondrous research skills.

Introduction

THE TURNING POINT IN golfer Ben Hogan's career came in January 1938, when he was still a struggling young golf pro trying to find a way to make a living in tournament competition. His game really wasn't that good, and his outgo of cash consistently outpaced his income.

Hogan and his wife, Valerie, traveled the golf circuit in a used car and, even though times were tough, they had managed to save fourteen hundred dollars for the specific purpose of giving Ben's tour golf one last go in 1938. It was now or never. They would hit the road with the fourteen hundred dollars and the idea was to go from tournament to tournament for as long as the cash held out.

By the time they got to Oakland, California, for another tournament a number of weeks later, the Hogans were down to their last eighty-six dollars. "He said that if we ran out of money we'd return home and I'd never hear about golf again," Valerie related in an interview after Ben's death in 1997. The dire circumstances wouldn't have been complete without a bad omen: Hogan waking up one morning at their motel and walking outside to the parking lot to discover that the two rear wheels on their car had been stolen. The thief had left the back of the car sitting on rocks.

As most anyone who has ever dug into Hogan's life knows, the story had a happy ending. Hogan finished second in that Oakland event and pocketed several hundred dollars, which he later called "the biggest check I'd ever seen in my life. And I'm quite sure it's the biggest check I'll ever see."

No longer did Hogan have to consider taking a nine-to-five job behind a desk or on an assembly line. Instead, it was simply the first step in a long and difficult struggle to try and become the best player the game has ever seen.

Some thought his effort was more of an obsession. But he garnered the respect of like-minded individuals who believed in his undying work ethic, his focus, and his unwavering belief that outplaying the competition began with outworking them on the practice range. Incredibly, the man who became perhaps the premier shotmaker in the history of the game never had a lesson. In his twenties, he totally rebuilt his game from scratch, all by himself, tearing himself down and putting back together the pieces, some in different places, kind of like the tinkering auto mechanic who takes apart an Edsel and puts back together a Rolls Royce.

The man probably came closest to absolute mastery of the golf swing. He loved to hit golf balls. As a child in Dublin, Texas, he would caddie at Glen Garden Country Club, hit balls until dark, then walk the seven miles home. This became his mantra: Outwork everyone.

Introduction

I T HAS ALWAYS BEEN difficult to compare athletes of different eras, and so it is in the discussion of golf's best player. Is it Jones? Hogan? Nicklaus? Woods? Consider some of the merits of Hogan's career résumé:

> He won sixty-three tour titles, third on the all-time list, with almost all of those victories packed into a fifteen-year stretch;

> He won the professional career Grand Slam despite playing in only one British Open, which he won in 1953 at age forty-one;

> Only four times has a PGA Tour player achieved double figures in victories in a calendar year: Hogan owns two of those achievements, having won thirteen times in 1946 and ten times two years later;

> He won nine professional majors, third on the all-time list. Consider the twists of fate that conspired against him, denying him dozens of opportunities to even play in majors at the peak of his career. He missed six U.S. Opens and four Masters because of either World War II or the injuries from his near-fatal automobile accident in 1949; he skipped numerous PGA Championships because of the format that required multiple thirty-six-hole days, a brutal torture to legs that never fully recovered from the accident. And Hogan had the unfortunate timing to play in an era where it was impossible to compete in both the PGA Championship and the British Open the same year. They

were often held on concurrent dates, and in the days before convenient transatlantic travel by plane, crossing the ocean on a steamship usually required seven days.

Hogan's crowning golf achievement came sixteen months after the accident when he captured the 1950 U.S. Open at Merion Golf Club in Ardmore, Pennsylvania. Doctors had told him after the wreck that he would most likely never walk again, but a year after the accident he tied Sam Snead for the seventy-two-hole lead at the Los Angeles Open, then won the Open five months later. Snead won eleven times that year, but it was Hogan who walked away with player of the year honors.

Said Doug Sanders: "That is why we are drawn to Ben Hogan. He overcame adversity and he showed us the possibility that we, too, can be victorious over adversity."

HOGAN'S PERSONAL REPUTATION WAS not as luminous as his playing career, however. He was said to be cold, aloof, distant, an expressionless golfing machine. Jimmy Demaret liked to explain Hogan's demeanor by saying: "He talks to me on every green. He always says, 'You're away.'"

Hogan was a man of few words. He usually avoided small talk, and he didn't exactly light up when reporters cornered him to ask questions. He wasn't what reporters today would call a quote machine. Hogan was brief and he was blunt, if he even spoke at all. For him, a conversation was giving a one-word answer to a yes-or-no question. Ask him another type of question, and an inquisitor would be fortunate to get a sentence or two, or, a stone-cold stare that felt like daggers but which friends explained away as shyness. He called it modesty. Whatever.

The silence could be deafening. In today's overexposed golf world of daily press conferences on-site at tournaments, television sound bites, endorsement overload, and twenty-four-hour radio sports babble, Hogan's Q rating would have been scratch—good if you're a golfer, bad if your agent is longing for some bang out of his 5-percent cut. Hogan's characteristic economy wasn't only in his ability to stretch a few bucks; it was also in his Calvin Coolidge-esque ability to say a whole lot with just a few words. The story goes that when someone told Coolidge that he had made a bet that he could get Coolidge to say more than two words, the U.S. president responded, "You lose." Hogan probably could have given that same answer to a dozen different questions he heard over the years: "Hey, Ben, how's 'bout me and my three buddies play a scramble against you and you spot us a stroke on the first six handicap holes?" Hogan: "You lose."

Hogan's reticence combined with his ability to cut to the quick when he spoke make his every spoken or written word something to be treasured. One of his instructionals, *Five Lessons: The Modern Fundamentals of Golf*, remains one of the best-selling golf books of all times, nearly fifty years after its original publication.

Hogan was profound not only when it came to discussing the golf swing and course management, he also had a good feel for what it took to be successful at anything, and he was able to convey those thoughts in a succinct manner easily understood by all. Hogan didn't have time for clichés; he probably detested them. What he did have was a deep appreciation for hard work and a love for life that often went unspoken, but which occasionally flowed out when he looked back over what he had been able to accomplish and the obstacles he had overcome along the way.

Quotable Hogan is by no means an exhaustive compilation of everything significant that Hogan said or wrote over his eighty-five years of life. As private as he was, some would even say reclusive, there surely is much about what Hogan said and wrote that has never been revealed and which never will be. Finding the many dozens of quotes used in this book proved to be an exercise that in one sense Hogan could have appreciated—many had to be dug out of the ground, or at least out of archives more than a half-century old. The result, it is hoped, is a unique compilation that brings the best and brightest of Hogan together in one place.

CHILDHOOD

> *The entire Hogan family was at home on the February morning in 1922 when Hogan's father, Chester, shot and killed himself with a .38 caliber handgun. Ben was nine at the time. Hogan had to contribute to the family's financial survival, and he did that by selling newspapers, then caddieing at Glen Garden Golf Course, which was a seven-mile walk one way. Though Hogan never publicly discussed his father's suicide and the impact it had upon him, some have suggested his life as a loner, and his unwavering resolve to overcome adversity, was forged by that traumatic event.*

After hours the caddies would go out to the practice range and dig a hole. Then we'd hit toward it from different places, playing nickel syndicates with the closest shot earning the nickels. I didn't usually take home that many nickels. Also, the caddie who had the shortest drive had to collect all the balls. I had to collect a lot of balls.[1]

—*discussing his game as a youngster, when he was a caddie*

1

HOGAN WAS A MAN POSSESSED, PROBABLY BECAUSE OF HIS CHILDHOOD AND ALL THE THINGS THAT HE WAS DENIED.[2]

> —*Jimmy Roberts, television sports commentator*

YOU HAVE TO THINK THAT, GOING THROUGH WHAT HE WENT THROUGH, GOLF GAVE HIM THE SOLITUDE AND PEACE THAT HE WAS YEARNING FOR.[3]

> —*Ben Crenshaw*

SOME OLD-TIMER SAID BEN HOGAN WOULD NEVER AMOUNT TO ANYTHING BECAUSE [AS A CHILD] ALL HE DID WAS RUN AROUND THE GOLF COURSE AND PICK UP GOLF BALLS.[4]

> —*Merle Hancock, family friend*

Young Ben Hogan, in front, is surrounded by his family: parents Chester and Clara, sister Princess, and older brother Royal; circa 1918. (United States Golf Association photo)

We didn't have much when I was little, but I've always remembered something my mother used to tell me. She said to never forget, no matter what, that I was as good as anybody else in the world. I think all I've ever done is try to live up to that.[5]

In 1924, I heard a boy could make sixty-five cents for carrying a bag eighteen holes at Glen Garden Country Club. That sounded good. I was making less selling papers until late at night. We had moved to Taylor Street near Seventh. It was seven miles to Glen Garden. I walked. There was no other way for me to get there.[6]

HE FELT SORRY FOR RICH KIDS WHO DIDN'T KNOW ADVERSI-
TY. HE FELT THAT ADVERSITY WAS THE MAKING OF A MAN.
WITHOUT IT, HE COULD NEVER ACCOMPLISH ANYTHING.[7]

> —*Frank Chirkinian, former*
> *executive producer for golf at CBS*

One, I didn't want to be a burden to my
mother. Two, I needed to put food on the
table. Three, I needed a place to sleep.[8]

> —*discussing the reasons for*
> *his motivation to be a success*

PRACTICE AND PREPARATION

There probably has never been a golfer with the single-minded dedication to practice and preparation to the extent that Hogan had. He followed his own prescription and usually conducted his work in complete solitude. There are dozens of tales of club members and other players sneaking out to the far end of the practice range or a seldom-used area on the golf course and hiding behind a tree, just to watch Hogan hit balls. Hogan could generally sense when he wasn't alone, however; frequently, he'd quietly gather up the range balls he'd hit and then depart, leaving the onlookers to themselves.

I always outworked everybody. Work never bothered me like it bothers some people. You can outwork the best player in the world.[1]

The secret is in the dirt.

> —*a frequently repeated answer by Hogan*
> *when asked about possessing a secret to the golf swing*

ALL I KNOW IS, I'VE SEEN NICKLAUS WATCH HOGAN PRACTICE. I'VE NEVER SEEN HOGAN WATCH NICKLAUS PRACTICE.[2]

> —*Tommy Bolt, golfer*

ONCE, AT THE TAM O'SHANTER, I SAW HIM HIT BALLS, AND THE BOY ON THE RANGE DIDN'T HAVE TO MOVE FIVE FEET TO PICK THEM UP.[3]

> —*Louise Suggs, golfer*

HE WASN'T THE MACHINE EVERYONE THOUGHT. HE JUST WORKED HARDER.[4]

> —*Valerie Hogan*

(It's) up to the player to dig it out on the practice tee by himself with trial and error. You can't do it in five minutes; you're lucky if you can do it in five years. It's a training process. Give it enough time and thought, anybody can break 80.[5]

The only thing a golfer needs is more daylight.[6]

⁓

Practice doesn't make perfect. Perfect practice makes perfect.

⁓

HOGAN'S SHOTS MADE SUCH A DISTINCTIVE SOUND. YOU COULD CLOSE YOUR EYES AND TELL WHERE HOGAN WAS ON THE PRACTICE RANGE.[7]

> —Bob Blyth, *at the time a Carnoustie member, recalling the 1953 British Open*

HE WASN'T GOING TO TELL YOU WHAT IT [SUCCESS] WAS. GET IT THE SAME WAY HE GOT IT, THE OLD-FASHIONED WAY, WORK FOR IT.[8]

> —Dave Kindred, *writer*

NO ONE WORKED OR PRACTICED HARDER THAN BEN.[9]

> —Byron Nelson

I would take longer on that first tee than I would any other place on the golf course. I was gearing my brain, taking a look at that fairway, taking three or four practice swings. A lot of people wondered what I was doing up there, why I didn't tee the ball up and hit it. I was organizing myself to play this round. I thought harder about that first shot than any shot I played. It set the tone for the day.[10]

—*Hogan's thoughts on the first tee before the start of a round*

HE HAD HIS CADDIE DOWN THERE ABOUT 180 YARDS, PRAC-
TICING THREE-IRONS. HE HIT HIM IN THE TOP OF THE HEAD
AND KNOCKED HIM DOWN, AND BEFORE HE COULD GET UP
HE HIT HIM TWICE MORE.[11]

—Paul Runyan, golfer

The more I practice, the luckier I get.[12]

Every day you miss practicing, it will take you one day
longer to be good.[13]

Preparing myself for tournaments and participating in
them consumed practically all my time and energies. Far
from leaving me with extra hours for teaching, it left me
only with the regret that the days were not longer so
that I could spend more time practicing and preparing.[14]

Playing the actual tournament is an anticlimax. Tournaments are won and lost in the preparation. Playing them is just going through the motions.[15]

~

I realize that in some ways I can be a demanding man and that some things are harder for certain people to do than I may appreciate, but it really cuts me up to watch some golfer sweating over his shots on the practice tee, throwing away his energy to no constructive purpose, nine times out of ten doing the same thing wrong he did years and years back when he first took up golf. . . . He's going to get worse and worse because he's going to get his bad habits more and more deeply ingrained.[16]

~

It was a great joy to improve. There wasn't enough daylight in the day for me. I always wished the days were longer so I could practice and work. I always enjoyed practicing more than playing because I could prove and disprove things.[17]

~

Don't simply tell a player what he's doing wrong. That's not much help. You must explain to him what he ought to be doing, why it is correct, and the result it produces—and work like blazes to get it across so that he really understands what you are talking about.[18]

~

I loved to hit balls and practice and key in on something, narrow the focus. That's a pleasure.[19]

I didn't hit that shot then. I'd been practicing that shot since I was twelve years old.[20]

—talking about his one-iron to the seventy-second green of the 1950 Open

I was one of the beginners of it. The other players used to laugh at me, going out there and practicing after I played, until I started winning; then they joined me.[21]

—Hogan's habit of practicing after he finished a round

I would practice one club until I thought I had it fine-tuned. Then I would move to another club. If I wasn't hitting a club well, I might hit the whole bag of balls to get it right. I would start with a nine-iron and go right through the set. The driver would be the last thing I hit. There might be a shot on a particular golf course that I would spend more time practicing.[22]

—Hogan on his practice routine

Practice until the calluses reach the bone. That'll cure you.[23]

—to a fellow pro who had complained about blisters forming under his calluses because of all the practice

A MAN OF FEW WORDS

> *Once, as he was waiting on the first tee for the start of a round, Hogan walked up to the player with whom he had been paired the day before. "I'm sorry I didn't speak to you yesterday," Hogan said. "But just so you're not surprised, I won't be saying anything today, either."*

Life's too short for me to go around explaining myself. A lot of people don't understand modesty. Not everybody wants publicity, you know.

I play golf with friends sometimes, but there are never friendly games.

HE COULD DISCUSS ALMOST ANY SUBJECT WITH YOU BECAUSE HE WAS THE BEST LISTENER. AS HE SAID, "PEOPLE WHO TALK ALL THE TIME DON'T LEARN ANYTHING BECAUSE YOU HAVE TO LISTEN, THAT'S HOW YOU LEARN," AND BELIEVE YOU ME, HE LISTENED.[1]

—*Valerie Hogan*

ABOUT ALL BEN EVER SAID IN A TOURNAMENT WAS "GOOD LUCK" ON THE (FIRST) TEE AND "YOU'RE AWAY" A FEW TIMES AFTER THAT.[2]

—*Sam Snead, golfer*

HOGAN WAS A BREED APART. HE WOULD NOT SAY HELLO TO HIS MOTHER IF SHE WERE OUT THERE.[3]

—*Ben Crenshaw,*
discussing Hogan's ability to concentrate

HE SAID VERY LITTLE ON THE GOLF COURSE, BUT HE SAID, "I'M GOING TO LET THE CLUBS SPEAK FOR ME." AND HE DID.[4]

—Sam Snead

HE WAS FAMOUS FOR SAYING NOTHING.[5]

—Gil Gross, CBS Radio news commentator

HE SAID "NICE SHOT" WHEN YOU HIT A NICE SHOT. AND HE DIDN'T SAY IT IF YOU DIDN'T REALLY HIT A NICE SHOT.[6]

—Jack Nicklaus, golfer

I TRAVEL WITH BEN HOGAN QUITE A LOT AND HE HAS A SET SPEECH FOR THESE OCCASIONS. IT GOES SOMETHING LIKE THIS: "THANKS FOR THE CHECK."[7]

—an unidentified pro retelling a story about Hogan, who was asked to say a few words after winning the Western Open

Before Hogan was able to achieve great things, most of them after age thirty, he had pretty much reinvented his entire golf game. Here he is at the 1941 Hershey Open. (United States Golf Association photo)

Because I didn't need a three.[8]

> —Hogan's answer when asked why he laid up
> at Augusta National Golf Club's par-five thirteenth

Shoot the lowest score.[9]

> —in response to a question from
> Nick Faldo on how to win the U.S. Open

There isn't a seven-iron shot at Merion.

> —Hogan's response to reporters at the 1950 U.S. Open
> as to why he didn't carry a seven-iron in his bag that week

THE HOGAN DEMEANOR

> The mere presence of Hogan could be intimidating. He was expressionless and possessed cold, piercing blue eyes, and his deportment on the course made it perfectly clear that he was strictly business.

Relax? How can anybody relax and play golf? You have to grip the club, don't you?[1]

Golf is two things: hitting a golf ball—
and hitting it properly—and the other
thing is playing golf. It's two different
animals entirely. You manage on a golf
course like you would a business. And
you manage one shot at a time.[2]

I'VE KNOWN HIM SINCE I WAS TWELVE YEARS OLD, AND IT'S
HARD TO UNDERSTAND HOW HE FEELS. I REALLY DON'T KNOW
ENOUGH ABOUT BEN TO KNOW WHAT MAKES HIM TICK.[3]

—*Byron Nelson*

Some people like to talk and some people like to keep their mouth shut. I always felt like when I went to a tournament that I was a guest of that club, and I tried to conduct myself accordingly.[4]

God, I miss tournament golf.[5]

I WAS SCARED EVERY TIME I WAS EVER AROUND HIM. IT WAS ONE OF THOSE THINGS—LOVE, RESPECT, AND FEAR, TOO. YOU COULD TALK TO THE MOST HARDENED OLD GUY OUT THERE AND HE'D TELL YOU THE SAME THING. THEY JUST USED TO SHAKE THEIR HEADS AT HIM.[6]

—*Ben Crenshaw*

HE WAS LIKE A SPHINX. EVEN IF HE LIKED YOU, HE COULD INTIMIDATE YOU.[7]

—*Dave Marr, golfer and TV commentator*

HE PLAYS WITH THE BURNING FRIGIDITY OF DRY ICE.[8]

—*Gene Sarazen, golfer*

BEN HOGAN IS THE MOST MERCILESS OF ALL THE MODERN GOLFERS.[9]

—*Gene Sarazen*

As you walk down the fairway of life, you must smell the roses, for you only get to play one round.

EVEN THE MOVEMENT OF CASTING THE CIGARETTE AWAY, READY
FOR THE NEXT SHOT, HAD A CAGNEY-ESQUE STYLE. THERE WAS
SOMETHING ABOUT EVERYTHING HE DID THAT WAS STYLISH.[10]

—Peter Alliss, TV golf analyst

YOU DIDN'T HAVE A CASUAL CONVERSATION WITH BEN. HE
LOOKED YOU IN THE PUPIL OF YOUR EYE RIGHT TO THE BACK OF
YOUR BRAIN.[11]

—Deane Beman, former PGA Tour commissioner

I DON'T BELIEVE BEN COULD HAVE CONCENTRATED THE WAY HE
DID IF HE DIDN'T SMOKE. IT GAVE HIM SOMETHING TO DO WHILE
HE WAS THINKING.[12]

—Ken Venturi

That's the most stupid question I've ever heard.[13]

*—berating a golf-ignorant reporter in the locker
room at Winged Foot during the 1959 U.S. Open*

THE GAME

This is a game of misses. The guy who misses the best is going to win.[1]

I liked playing better than teaching.[2]

I CAN TELL YOU NO ONE, NO ONE, LOVED GOLF MORE THAN BEN HOGAN.[3]

—*Valerie Hogan*

You expect to miss a few shots, but it's the stupid shots that cause you to lose tournaments.[4]

I have loved playing the game and practicing it. Whether my schedule for the following day called for a tournament round or merely a trip to the practice tee, the prospect that there was going to be golf in it made me feel privileged and extremely happy, and I couldn't wait for the sun to come up the next morning so that I could get out on the course again.[5]

One of the greatest pleasures in golf—I can think of nothing that truly compares with it unless it is watching a well-played shot streak for the flag—is the sensation a golfer experiences at the instant he contacts the ball flush and correctly. . . . Not even the best golfer can hit the ball this well on every shot, for golf, in essence, is a game of misses.[6]

You can hit your shots great and still shoot 80 every day because of poor management. The shots are 30 percent of the game. Judgment is 70 percent.[7]

—press briefing at the 1953 Masters

Golf is 20 percent skill and 80 percent management.[8]

I never worked out. If you hit enough balls, you'll get strong.[9]

There's no such thing as one good shot in big-time golf. They all have to be good—and for seventy-two holes.[10]

HE TOLD ME, "I DIDN'T HIT ONE SHOT THAT TURNED OUT THE WAY I WANTED IT TO. IF YOU CAN PLAY A ROUND OF GOLF AND HIT THREE SHOTS THAT TURN OUT THE WAY YOU WANT, YOU'VE HAD A GOOD ROUND OF GOLF."[11]

—*Dan Jenkins, writer and Hogan friend*

I have always thought of golf as the best of all games—the most interesting, the most demanding, the most rewarding. I have found the game to be, in all factualness, a universal language wherever I have traveled at home or abroad.[12]

I love to play in tournaments. You have to be in it to enjoy it. At least, I do. I get my kicks playin' in a golf tournament.[13]

⌒

Up to a considerable point, as I see it, there's nothing difficult about golf—nothing. I see no reason, truly, why the average golfer, if he goes about it intelligently, shouldn't play in the 70s—and I mean by playing the type of shots a fine golfer plays. . . . In my opinion, the average golfer underrates himself.[14]

⌒

While a world war raged, Hogan emerged as an American sporting hero. This is Hogan pictured signing autographs at the 1942 Hale America National Open, which he won and many still count as his fifth U.S. Open title. (United States Golf Association photo)

Perhaps the only true mystery to golf is the essential magnetism the game possesses which makes so many of us, regardless of discouragement, never quite turn in our trench coats and magnifying glasses and stop our search for the answers.[15]

~

The average golfer's problem is not so much a lack of ability as it is a lack of knowing what he should do.[16]

~

When I'm hitting the ball where I want, hard and crisply—when anyone is—it's a joy that very few people experience.[17]

~

Winning golf is a matter of touch. It's something you work at and try to develop, but you don't develop it. It just comes to you. It's the difference between a first-rate golfer and the fellow who scores good once in a while. Once you've got the touch, you're set. Even if you make a bad shot now and then, you know you've still got it. The good golfer has got the touch. He knows he can do it.[18]

⌒

The drive. It governs the nature of the entire hole. It tells you whether you have problems or don't.[19]

—when asked what he considered
the most important shot in golf

⌒

I try to find out some-
thing new about golf
every day.[20]

THE SWING

Is it possible that a person could win sixty-three tour titles and never take a lesson? Because Hogan did just that, his intimate knowledge of the golf swing was said to be unparalleled. Before he retired from competitive golf, he wrote Five Lessons: the Modern Fundamentals of Golf, *which has sold more copies than any other golf-instruction book in history.*

I don't teach. It's all there in the book. Nothing about the swing has changed.[1]

⌒

The ultimate judge of your swing is the flight of the ball.[2]

⌒

Hogan looking sharp, in more ways than one. (United States Golf Association photo)

Reverse every natural instinct and do the opposite of what you are inclined to do, and you will probably come very close to having a perfect golf swing.[3]

NEVER HAS THERE BEEN A GOLFER WHO INFLUENCED THE
SWING MORE THAN BEN HOGAN. IN FACT, IF YOU NAMED
THE NEXT THREE GUYS (TOGETHER), THEY WOULDN'T BE AS
INFLUENTIAL AS BEN HOGAN.[4]

—Johnny Miller, golfer and TV golf commentator

You don't hook a ball because you have a strong right hand. You hook it because you have a weak left.[5]

This can be stated categorically: It is utterly impossible for any golfer to play good golf without a swing that will repeat.[6]

I hate a hook. It nauseates me. I could vomit when I see one. It's like a rattlesnake in your pocket.[7]

On every golf course there are certain shots you have to hit in certain places, and if you can't hit them, forget it.[8]

My advice to the beginning golfer is to go ahead and hit the ball as hard as he can right from the start. . . . Later on he can straighten out his hooks and slices with minor alterations to his swing.[9]

—from his plans to publish an instruction book, Power Golf

You simply cannot bypass the fundamentals in golf any more than you can sit down at the piano without a lesson and rip off the score of *My Fair Lady*.[10]

⌒

I STUDIED HIS EVERY MOVE AND ANALYZED HIS CAREER. . . . I STILL STUDY HIS BOOK LIKE IT'S A TRUE SCRIPTURE.[11]

—*Johnny Miller*

⌒

I don't believe anybody else can hit a straight ball. You only hit a straight ball by accident. The ball is going to move left or right every time you hit it, so you had better make it go one way or the other. Make it go one way or the other and you effectively double your target area.[12]

—*when asked whether he ever hit a straight ball on purpose*

⌒

There's no such thing as a natural golf swing.[13]

⌒

Ultimately, you have to be able to fix your own swing from one shot to the next on the golf course, where there is nobody there to help you. You don't need any help if you are going to play tournaments. If you need help, you get off the tour.[14]

—*his response to a question whether he would avail himself the use of a sports psychologist, as many modern-day players do*

⌒

I can't recall ever having a golf lesson, but I've learned thousands of things by watching good players play golf.[15]

⌒

There is no similarity between golf and putting; they are two different games, one played in the air, and the other on the ground.[16]

⌒

I'm telling you I could spend ten minutes with you and guarantee that you'll never hook another ball again—unless you want to.[17]

Some things you try don't work out, so you just go back and find something that does work.[18]

CHARACTERISTICS OF A CHAMPION

I wanted to succeed in anything I've ever done.[1]

⌣

I'm the sole judge of my standards.

—*press briefing at the U.S. Open, June 1951*

⌣

There's no reason in the world why a man can't birdie every hole.[2]

—*Hogan's response when asked why he was still practicing after a round of 64 that included ten birdies*

⌣

I liked to win, but more than anything I loved to play the way I wanted to play.[3]

⌒

There's a great difference between intelligence and wisdom. You might have a college sheepskin, but that doesn't make you educated.

⌒

HE DID WHATEVER IT TOOK TO GET WHERE HE WANTED TO GO, WHICH WAS PLAYING GOLF FOR A LIVING. HE HAD DEVELOPED A LOVE FOR GOLF AND AN ADDICTION FROM THE POSITIVE FEELINGS HE GOT FROM SUCCEEDING AT IT, AND NOTHING WAS GOING TO STOP HIM.[4]

—*Curt Sampson, Hogan biographer*

⌒

THERE WAS SOMETHING ABOUT HOGAN. HE KNEW HOW TO WIN, AND HE WAS ABSOLUTELY COOL AND UNFLAPPABLE. IT SEEMED LIKE THE GREATER THE PRESSURE ON HIM, THE BETTER HE PERFORMED.[5]

—William Nack, writer

HE DIDN'T KNOW WHAT QUIT WAS. HE DIDN'T EVEN KNOW THAT EXISTED.[6]

—Sam Snead

IF HE WASN'T A GENIUS, HE WAS CERTAINLY THE HARDEST-WORKING, MOST DEEPLY FOCUSED PLAYER WHO EVER LIVED.[7]

—Chris Fowler, ESPN

HE PICKED HIS CLUBS OUT OF THE BAG WITH THE CONFI-
DENCE OF A SURGEON SELECTING SHARP INSTRUMENTS, AND
EVERY CUT HE TOOK AT THE BALL WAS JUST DEEP ENOUGH
TO DRAW THE BLOOD OF THE ENTIRE FIELD WHICH OPPOSED
HIM. . . . HE HAS REDUCED THE GAME TO A MORE EXACT SCI-
ENCE THAN EVEN THE EXPERTS THOUGHT POSSIBLE.[8]

—Pinehurst Outlook

HE WAS AS CLOSE TO PERFECTION AS ANY HUMAN BEING HAS
EVER BEEN HITTING A GOLF BALL.[9]

—Dave Marr

HE SAID THERE'S THREE WAYS TO BEAT A PERSON. YOU OUT-
WORK THEM, YOU OUTTHINK THEM AND, IF THAT DOESN'T
WORK, YOU INTIMIDATE THEM.[10]

—Ken Venturi

A beaming Hogan surrounded by his favorite kind of hardware. (United States Golf Association photo)

TO THIS DAY I'VE NEVER SEEN ANYONE HIT A GOLF BALL
WITH THAT KIND OF PRECISION AND CONTROL OF DISTANCE
AND ACCURACY AS BEN HOGAN DID. SAM SNEAD WAS A
CLOSE SECOND.[11]

—Tom Weiskopf, golfer

HOGAN HAD NO WEAKNESSES THROUGHOUT THE BAG.[12]

—Dan Jenkins

BEN'S STANDARDS WERE FAR ABOVE EVERYONE ELSE'S. HE'D
TRY AND PUT HIS TEE SHOT IN A TEN-TO-TWELVE-FOOT AREA
DOWN ONE SIDE OF THE FAIRWAY BECAUSE IT SET UP A
BETTER ANGLE FOR HIS APPROACH TO THE GREEN. THE
REST OF US JUST WANTED TO KEEP IT IN THE FAIRWAY.[13]

—Charles Coody, golfer

IF HE'D PLAYED TODAY, WITH THIS EQUIPMENT, HEAVEN KNOWS WHAT HE WOULD HAVE SCORED. TODAY, PEOPLE ARE WANTING TO WORK LESS IN LIFE AND GET MORE. AND HERE WAS A MAN THAT SET THE WORK ETHIC IN GOLF. IF HE WAS OUT THERE TODAY ON THE PGA TOUR, OUTWORKING PEOPLE LIKE HE DID AND PLAYING WITH THESE CLUBS . . . IT'S A SCARY THOUGHT.[14]

—*Gary Player, golfer*

If you can't outplay them, outwork them.[15]

IT WAS THE SELF-SATISFACTION OF ACCOMPLISHMENT. THAT'S WHAT HE HAD WITHIN HIMSELF.[16]

—*Jack Fleck, golfer*

HE BROUGHT SOMETHING TO THE GAME NO ONE EVER HAS. HE SHOWED YOU COULD MAKE YOURSELF A GREAT PLAYER.[17]

—*Arnold Palmer, golfer*

This card is wrong. It's 148 yards to the middle.[18]

—*spoken before filming a segment of* Shell's Wonderful World of Golf *while eyeballing a par-three hole listed on the scorecard as 152 yards to the middle of the green. The hole was remeasured. It was 148 yards.*

All other things being equal, greens break to the west.[19]

THE HOGAN REPUTATION

Your name is the most important thing you own. Don't ever do anything to disgrace or cheapen it.[1]

〜

I would like to be known as a gentleman first and next as a golfer. That's all.[2]

〜

NO ONE EVER PLAYED THE GAME LIKE MR. HOGAN, AND NO HUMAN HAS EVER COME AS CLOSE TO CONTROLLING THE BALL AS PERFECTLY AS HE DID.[3]

—Ben Crenshaw

THROUGHOUT THE HISTORY OF CIVILIZATION, THERE HAVE BEEN SYLLABLES OF TERROR HANDED DOWN FROM GENERA-TION TO GENERATION. GERONIMO, FOR EXAMPLE, COULD BE COUNTED ON TO EMPTY ONE FORT AFTER ANOTHER IN THE OLD WEST. ATTILA WOULD STRIKE AS MUCH NAKED FEAR AS THE PLAGUE. IN THE LITTLER WORLD OF GOLF, HOGAN ELICITED MUCH THE SAME EFFECT. NOTHING COULD PARA-LYZE A FIELD OF GOLFERS AS MUCH AS THIS WHISPERED COL-LECTION OF SYLLABLES. STRONG MEN BOGEYED WHEN THEY HEARD THIS DREADED NAME. SAM SNEAD ONCE SAID THE ONLY THING HE FEARED ON A GOLF COURSE WAS LIGHT-NING—AND BEN HOGAN.[4]

—Jim Murray, writer

FOR AS LONG AS THE GAME IS PLAYED, THE NAME BEN HOGAN WILL HAVE A UNIQUE FASCINATION FOR ALL TRUE GOLFERS, AS WELL AS COMMANDING THE DEEPEST RESPECT. FOR THOSE WHO FOLLOW GOLF CLOSELY, HE WAS THE TOTAL EMBODIMENT OF WHAT A GREAT PLAYER SHOULD BE.[5]

—Ben Crenshaw

I HAD A GREAT DEAL OF RESPECT FOR HOGAN. WHEN I FIRST PLAYED WITH HIM, I DIDN'T THINK I'D EVER MEET ANYBODY WHO STRUCK THE BALL AS WELL, WHO KNEW WHAT WAS GOING TO HAPPEN TO IT.[6]

—Arnold Palmer

HE'S THE ONLY GOLFER IN THE WORLD I'M SCARED OF.[7]

—Lloyd Mangrum, golfer

YOU CAN'T BEAT HIM, SO WHAT ARE YOU GOING TO DO
ABOUT IT?[8]

*—quote from an unidentified player
after Hogan won his fourth Colonial title*

BEN EXPLAINED HE IS NOT PLAYING WELL AND THAT HE WAS
A LITTLE WARY OF EXPOSING HIMSELF IN A TOURNAMENT AS
BIG AS THE JULY AFFAIR, BECAUSE IF HE DID NOT FINISH HIGH
UP, IT CONCEIVABLY COULD AFFECT THE SALES OF THE GOLF
CLUBS THAT BEAR HIS NAME.

HE FURTHER EXPLAINED THAT HE WAS MAKING A SERI-
OUS EFFORT TO POPULARIZE THE CLUBS BY OTHER SALES-
MANSHIP LINES, AND HE FELT THAT HE OWED IT TO STOCK-
HOLDERS IN THE COMPANY NOT TO RISK HURTING A GOOD
PRODUCT BY LOSING WHILE PLAYING WITH THEM.[9]

*—paraphrasing Hogan's decision to turn down an
invitation to play in the Brussels World Fair golf tournament*

The Hogan Reputation

I HELD HOGAN IN GREAT RESPECT AND, TO SOME DEGREE, SOME AWE.[10]

—*Arnold Palmer*

I DON'T GET IN AWE OF TOO MANY PEOPLE, BUT JUST TO BE ABLE TO SAY I MET HIM WAS SOMETHING. THE MEETING MEANT A LOT TO ME BECAUSE THERE ARE ONLY A COUPLE OF GOLFERS YOU CAN PUT UP THERE ON A PEDESTAL, JACK NICKLAUS BEING ONE AND BEN HOGAN THE OTHER.[11]

—*Greg Norman, golfer*

PERHAPS NO OTHER PLAYER HAD THE SAME IMPACT ON THE WAY PEOPLE APPROACHED THE PLAYING OF THE GAME AS MR. HOGAN. THE HOGAN MYSTIQUE BECAME PART OF THE ALLURE OF GOLF.[12]

—*Tim Finchem, PGA Tour commissioner*

THE ACCIDENT

On February 2, 1949, on their way back to Fort Worth from a tournament in Phoenix, Arizona, Ben and Valerie Hogan were driving on a two-lane, fog-shrouded road in Van Horn, Texas, about 150 miles east of El Paso. From out of nowhere, they were met by an oncoming Greyhound bus that was attempting to pass another car. With a bridge abutment preventing Hogan from swerving onto the shoulder, he dove to his right and not only saved his own life—the force of the collision impaled the steering wheel through the front seat—but Valerie's as well. She was largely unhurt; he sustained serious injuries to his shoulder, hip, and pelvis, but both legs were damaged to the point where some doctors questioned whether he would ever walk again.

Watch out for buses.

—Hogan's response to reporters at a press briefing announcing the inauguration of the Hogan Tour, when asked what advice he had for struggling young players

The Accident

I was driving slowly in my lane when I saw four head-lights. I tried to get off the highway. There was a culvert, so I couldn't get over very far. I turned as far as I could and was hit. I was told later it was a bus.[1]

—recalling the accident in court testimony where bus driver Alvin Logan was charged with aggravated assault with a motor vehicle

I don't think the doctors know.[2]

—when asked about the possibility of playing golf after his accident

I always had an idea that some people didn't like me . . . that the majority of the people didn't like me. Then, after the accident, when I received all those wonderful telegrams and letters and flowers from people, I realized I was wrong about the people. That's when I changed. My frame of mind became different.[3]

PUBLIC SENTIMENT WOULD NOT COME BEN'S WAY UNTIL
AFTER HE LOOKED INTO THE FACE OF DEATH ONE FOGGY
MORNING ON A TWO-LANE TEXAS ROAD.[4]

—*Chris Fowler*

PEOPLE AROUND THE NEWSPAPER NEVER DID THINK IT WAS
GOING TO BE FATAL. THEY JUST COULDN'T IMAGINE BEN
HOGAN BEING KILLED IN A CAR ACCIDENT. HE WOULDN'T
ALLOW IT.[5]

—*Blackie Sherrod, writer*

LADY, HE WON'T BE NEEDING GOLF STICKS ANYMORE.[6]

—*a policeman's response to Valerie Hogan, who
asked him to pick up Ben's golf clubs after they
were scattered all over the roadway following the accident*

BEN'S CLUBS WERE NOT INJURED.[7]

—*last line of a magazine report
on Hogan's automobile crash*

I just put my head down and dived across Valerie's lap, like I was diving into a pool of water.[8]

I GUESS HE SAVED HIS OWN LIFE BY SAVING VALERIE'S.[9]

—*Ken Venturi*

WE ALL WENT TO THE CHAPEL TO PRAY BECAUSE WE ALL THOUGHT IT COULD BE TOO LATE.[10]

—*Valerie Hogan*

I can enjoy the little things in life now a lot more than I used to.[11]

—*discussing the accident's impact on his life*

If I ever get out of here, I'm going to be more aware of people—and their kindness to me.[12]

THE COMEBACK

If walking was in question, recovering to the point where he would be able to play professional golf was almost a pointless debate. But less than a year after the accident, he entered the Los Angeles Open and tied for the lead after seventy-two holes. (He lost to Sam Snead in a playoff.) A few months later, at Merion Golf Club in suburban Philadelphia, he won the U.S. Open to complete one of the most phenomenal comeback stories in golf history.

They say I'm going to be all right, but you have to play tournament golf to know what it is. Sure, I'll probably be all right to go downtown and sit in an office every day. It's like Joe DiMaggio. They tell him, "You're all right—go ahead and run on that heel." Maybe he looks all right, but it's probably hurting him like the devil.[1]

I don't know yet if I'll ever be able to go back to tournament play. Only time will tell and it may be a long time.[2]

I'm going to try. It's going to be a long haul, and in my own mind, I don't think that I'll ever get back the playing edge I had last year. You work for perfection all your life, and then something like this happens. My nervous system has been all shot by this, and I don't see how I can readjust it to competitive golf. But you can bet I'll be back there swinging.[3]

THE MOST INCREDIBLE COMEBACK IN THE HISTORY OF
SPORTS.[4]

—Dan Jenkins, talking about
Hogan's victory at the 1950 U.S. Open

IT WAS ONE OF THE GREAT COMEBACKS AND GETTING OFF
THE DECK, OF ANY CHAMPION IN HISTORY, OF ANY SPORT.[5]

—Ben Crenshaw

THAT WAS PROBABLY ONE OF THE GREATEST COMEBACKS IN
THE TWENTIETH CENTURY BECAUSE THIS MAN WAS GIVEN UP
FOR DEAD.[6]

—Sid Dorfman, writer

BEN, YOU HAVE TO HURRY AND GET WELL BECAUSE THESE
TOURNAMENTS DON'T MEAN MUCH WITHOUT YOU. I DON'T
PLAY GOLF, I'M JUST A DUMP [TRUCK] DRIVER, BUT I READ
ABOUT YOU IN THE PAPERS. IT JUST ISN'T THE SAME WITHOUT
YOU IN THE TOURNAMENTS.[7]

*—excerpt from a letter to Ben Hogan, delivered to him
in the hospital as he was recuperating from his injuries*

I'm awfully tired. I wish I didn't have to
play tomorrow. Rather than that, I wish
he'd won the tournament today.[8]

*—after Sam Snead tied Hogan following seventy-two
holes of regulation at the Los Angeles Open, thereby
forcing an eighteen-hole playoff the next day*

It's going to be that way until I can play the kind of golf I want.[9]

—*in response to a question as to whether golf was foremost in his mind*

One thing for sure, I'll never teach again. I tried that once and that was enough.[10]

—*Hogan's response when asked what he'd do if he couldn't play tournament golf*

It may be special to everyone else, but not to me. . . . I enjoyed every tournament I played in. I didn't enjoy my play sometimes, but I enjoyed the tournaments. I don't really have a favorite.[11]

—*when asked if his victory at the 1950 U.S. Open, following his auto accident, was the most significant of his career*

MAJOR CHAMPIONSHIPS

The greater the stakes, the more Hogan was able to raise the level of his game. He won nine professional majors, the third best mark in history behind Jack Nicklaus and Walter Hagen. But Hogan also was the victim of unfortunate circumstances. He missed the opportunity to compete in another few dozen majors because of World War II, injuries suffered from the automobile accident, and scheduling conflicts that prohibited players from competing in both the PGA Championship and the British Open.

The 1950 Open was my biggest win. It proved I could still play.[1]

You talk about something running up and down your spine.[2]

> —Hogan's comment regarding his second-nine 30 in the third round of the 1967 Masters, when he was fifty-four years old

Enclosed is my entry for the Open, with the hope that I will be able to play. Up to now I haven't taken a swing, but miracles may happen. Would you please do me a favor and not release my entry? If I can play I should like it to be a surprise.[3]

> —excerpt from Hogan's note to USGA executive director Joseph C. Dey in the spring of 1949. Hogan withdrew from that Open before the qualifying rounds.

I find myself waking up at night thinking about that shot right today. . . . There isn't a month that goes by that that doesn't cut my guts out.[4]

> —Hogan's recollection of his third shot at the par-five seventeenth at Cherry Hills in the final round of the 1960 Open. His shot spun off the green and into the water, depriving him of his chance to win a record fifth U.S. Open.

It jarred my teeth every time I hit the ball.[5]
—commenting about Carnoustie,
where he won the British Open in 1953

I think I played the best nine holes of my life on those holes. I don't think I came close to missing a shot.[6]
—discussing his third round of the 1967 Masters,
fourteen years after his last major victory

I have wondered what Willie Anderson and Bobby Jones said when they won their fourth Opens. I would like to say God must be with you to win the Open.[7]
—after winning his fourth U.S. Open

HOGAN'S PROGRESS OVER THE AUGUSTA ARBORETUM WAS AS SHOWY AS A BROADWAY SHOWGIRL STRUTTING ALONG FIFTH AVENUE ON EASTER SUNDAY MORNING, LEADING HER PEKINGESE ON A SILVER CORD.[8]

—a Golf World *editorial about*
Hogan's victory at the 1953 Masters

BEN WAS JUST TOO GOOD FOR ALL THE OTHERS AND TOO
GOOD FOR THE TOUGHEST COURSE HE EVER PLAYED. . . . HE
DID CONSIDER HIS CLOSING 67 AT OAKLAND HILLS, WHICH
WON HIM THE TITLE, AS THE GREATEST SINGLE ROUND HE
HAS EVER PLAYED IN COMPETITION.[9]

—Golf World *editorial, after Hogan's win at the U.S. Open*

If I had to play this course every week, I'd get into
another business.

*—in response to the difficulty of Oakland Hills
Country Club for the 1951 U.S. Open*

I'm glad that I brought this course, this monster, to its
knees.

*—comments during the prize presentation after a
final-round 67 at Oakland Hills, considered one of the
great rounds in golf history, to win the 1951 U.S. Open*

THERE IS NO DOUBT THAT HOGAN IS THE GREATEST GOLFER OF
HIS TIME. HIS RECORD IS LACKING IN ONLY ONE PARTICULAR. IF
HIS HEALTH PERMITS, HE NEEDS TO WIN ON THE SAND DUNES
OF SCOTLAND OR ENGLAND, TO COMPLETE WHAT MIGHT EASI-
LY BE THE GREATEST RECORD IN ALL GOLF HISTORY.[10]

> —Golf World, *two years before Hogan won the
> British Open to complete a career Grand Slam*

IT WAS FLAWLESS, HIGH-POWERED GOLF, THE LIKE OF WHICH
HAS NOT BEEN SEEN FOR A LONG TIME, EVEN IN THIS HOME
OF GOLF.[11]

> —John MacAdam, *writing about the 1953 British Open*

There's nothing I want to prove to myself.[12]
—*during the announcement to play in that year's British Open.*

The galleries won't be for me. They'll want one of
their own to win.[13]

> —*expressing to fellow golfer Frank Stranahan what proved
> to be needless concern before playing the 1953 British Open*

We've made a mistake! Don't unpack. We're going back home![14]

> —*an outraged Hogan to Valerie after arriving at their Scotland hotel to find that their room didn't have a private bath for him to soak his injured legs in. They ended up staying at a mansion with a spare bedroom and private bath.*

This is the hardest course I've ever played. I'm so grateful that I can't explain it in words. This sort of thing brings tears to my eyes. I have a tough skin but a soft spot in my heart, and things like this find that soft spot.[15]

> —*discussing his British Open victory at Carnoustie and ensuing welcome-home celebrations*

I just wait until those things come around and if I'm feeling good, I play. As for trying to beat somebody's record or something, I don't go for that. Sure, I'd like to win a fifth Open; I'd like to win ten of them.[16]

I would be satisfied if I never won another tournament.

> —*from his comments after winning the 1951 Masters*

It (the breeze at Augusta's par-three twelfth) was always . . . a guessing game. One day Bob Rosburg was playing right in front of me. He was on the twelfth tee. We finished eleven and walked over there. The wind was coming against him over those trees, coming down from the other course over there, Augusta Country Club. He hit a four-iron and the wind let up a little bit and he went clear over onto the other golf course. He teed up another ball, with the same club, hit it the same way and dropped it on the green.[17]

—*discussing the wind at Augusta National*

Hogan blasting out of trouble at the 1954 U.S. Open at Baltusrol. (United States Golf Association photo)

HOGAN'S HUMOR

If this goes through the green, I'm going to bury the club in your forehead![1]

—addressing caddie Cecil Timms at the 1953 British Open after Timms convinced him to switch clubs before hitting an approach shot through changing winds

When I'm playing golf, that's the most important thing in the world to me. It's a pleasure for me to work. I'm no Bob Hope. I try to produce good golf shots. I'm a bad joke teller.[2]

⁓

Better read it again.[3]

> —Hogan's response to a club member who remarked how he read Hogan's instructional book, Five Lessons, *but that it didn't help much*

⁓

Selecting a stroke is like selecting a wife; to each his own.[4]

~

Hit the ball up to the hole . . . You meet a better class of person there.[5]

~

If I had my game and Demaret's personality, I'd really be something.[6]

~

In 1980 a Dallas Morning News *columnist wrote a column about Hogan that included a reference to Hogan's canine companion, Max, which the columnist referred to as "the club dog (sitting) obediently while Hogan strikes ball after ball." Reading this, Hogan dashed off a letter to the columnist, showing a sense of humor that not many people knew Hogan had in him:*

There is a problem, however, stemming from your article in that Max is suing me for contributory negligence. You recalled that you called Max "the club dog." Everyone, including Max, knows he is not a dog but that he is President, Chairman of the Board, and protector of the club's membership.

I have explained to Max that this article was written unbeknown to me, but he will not accept that. Our relationship is rather strained in that when I speak to him now he wags his tail very slightly, whereas in the past he would give me a vigorous waggle. Also, he has stopped watching me practice. This, of course, really puts me down since he was my last gallerite [sic].

I will try to settle this suit out of court for a few quarter pounders, but if Max refuses and requests a jury trial, I am positive I will lose this case and he will be awarded the whole herd of Santa Gertrudis from the King Ranch.[7]

Why don't you hit them closer to
the hole?[8]

*—Hogan's response to a touring pro who
complained he was having trouble with his putting*

You know what I'm afraid of? I'm
afraid I'll be riding along in that big
black car and somebody over there
on the side of the street will say,
"Who's that lug there?"[9]

*—discussing the celebration and
ticker-tape parade in New York City*

TRIBUTES AND ACCOLADES

> *Someone once said of a dominant athlete: "He may not be in a class of his own, but when they take roll, there aren't many names called." So it was with Hogan, whose standard of excellence was generally considered to be unequaled by anyone who had ever played the game.*

HOGAN WAS THE GOLFER THAT ALL OTHER GOLFERS MEASURED THEMSELVES AGAINST.[1]

—*William Nack, writer*

WHEN EVERYTHING IS GOING AGAINST THIS GUY, THE OTHERS HAVE TO HAVE EVERYTHING GOING THEIR WAY TO BEAT HIM. IF BEN GETS THINGS GOING HIS WAY, IT'S NO CONTEST.[2]

—*Claude Harmon, golfer*

83

WHEN YOU BEAT THAT GUY, BROTHER, YOU'VE DONE SOMETHING.[3]

> —*Sam Snead, after beating Hogan in a playoff for the 1954 Masters*

IN THE AMERICAN SCHEME OF THINGS, CERTAIN THINGS ARE REGARDED AS GILT-EDGED INVESTMENTS—LIKE UNITED STATES STEEL, AMERICAN TEL & TEL, AND BEN HOGAN.[4]

> —Golf World

I THINK HE GAVE TO GOLF WHAT ASTAIRE GAVE TO DANCING. HE'S THE MAN BY WHOM EVERYONE IS MEASURED.[5]

> —*Dave Marr*

HE'S BEATEN OUT THE BOYS AND THE MEN HALF AND TWO-THIRDS HIS AGE, IN A YOUNG MAN'S PROFESSION, AND DONE IT IN A MANNER THAT LEAVES LITTLE MEANING TO SECOND PLACE.[6]

> —*from an editorial in the* New York Times

SOME THINK BEN HOGAN WAS THE GREATEST GOLFER OF ALL TIME. BUT WHAT THERE IS NO DEBATE ABOUT IS THAT HE WAS THE GREATEST GOLFER OF ANOTHER TIME. AT A TIME WHEN WE KNOW TOO MUCH ABOUT EVERY KIND OF CELEBRITY, AND ESPECIALLY THE SPORTS CELEBRITY, INCLUDING THE NAME OF EVERY WOMAN THEY DATED BEFORE THEY GOT MARRIED AND EVEN THE NAMES OF EVERY WOMAN THEY DATED WHILE THEY WERE MARRIED, HOGAN SEEMS AS IF HE LIVED IN ANOTHER WORLD.[7]

—Gil Gross

ARNOLD PALMER AND JACK NICKLAUS ARE GREAT. BUT . . . THEY COULDN'T CARRY BEN'S JOCKSTRAP. ONLY WAY YOU BEAT BEN WAS IF GOD WANTED YOU TO.[8]

—Tommy Bolt

I'LL NEVER WIN AN OPEN UNTIL HE RETIRES.[9]

—Sam Snead, who never did win a U.S. Open

WHO SHALL SAY HE IS NOT THE BEST OF ALL TIME?[10]

—*Leonard Crawley, writer*

HE WAS THE GREATEST SHOTMAKER EVER. JACK NICKLAUS WAS THE GREATEST WINNER. BUT NOBODY HIT SHOTS LIKE HOGAN.[11]

—*Frank Luksa, writer*

I WOULD HAVE HAD TWICE THE CAREER I HAD IF I WOULD HAVE BEEN SMART ENOUGH NOT TO TRY TO FIGURE OUT AND PLAY LIKE BEN HOGAN BUT LIKE GARDNER DICKINSON.[12]

—*Gardner Dickinson, well-known golfer who emulated Hogan in some ways, right down to the Hogan cap*

WHEN YOU TALK GREAT CHAMPIONS, HIS NAME COMES FIRST.[13]

—*Mark Brooks, golfer*

Hogan shows actor Glenn Ford some of the finer points of the golf swing. Ford portrayed Hogan in the movie Follow the Sun. (*United States Golf Association photo*)

HE'S THE STANDARD OF EXCELLENCE AGAINST WHICH WE ALL MEASURED OURSELVES.[14]

—*Peter Thomson, golfer*

HOGAN WAS THE HERO OF THE DADS WHO FATHERED THE BABY BOOM. THEY WISHED FOR JUST ONE ROUND WITH THE MAN. THEY DEVOURED HIS BOOKS ON GOLF. THEY STUDIED HIS SWING. BUT FINALLY, THEY WERE JUST SATISFIED WITH BEING ABLE TO WATCH WITHOUT HOPE OF EMULATING, BEING HAPPY ENOUGH TO BE IN THE PRESENCE OF PERFEC-TION, MUCH AS WE ADMIRE A SUNSET WITHOUT ANY ASPIRA-TION TO CREATE ONE OURSELVES. SOMETIMES IT'S ENOUGH TO ADMIRE. IN A WORLD THAT PLAYS TO OUR FANTASIES OF BEING ABLE TO DO WHATEVER WE WANT WITHOUT PRACTICE OR THE PATIENCE TO DEVELOP A SKILL, EVEN IN THIS WORLD, THERE IS SOMETIMES SOMEONE WHO IS SO GOOD AT SOME-THING THAT WITNESSING THEIR REALITY BESTS OUR FANTASY. IN A WORLD WHERE THE BRAGGING OFTEN DROWNS OUT EVEN THE CHEERING CROWD, THE SOUND OF A QUIET MAN CAN BE TRULY DEAFENING.[15]

—*Gil Gross*

THE WORLD COLLECTION OF BRILLIANT GOLFERS BECAME LESSER MEN IN THE FACE OF THIS INVINCIBLE MIRACLE MAN.[16]

—Desmond Hackett, writer

YOU HAVE PROVED TO THE YOUTH OF THE NATION THAT OPPORTUNITY HAS NOT BECOME EXTINCT IF THEY'RE WILLING TO CHOOSE THEIR FIELD AND DOGGEDLY STICK TO THEIR WORK. YOU HAVE PROVED TO THE MORE MATURE AMONG US THAT ALL SEEMINGLY INSURMOUNTABLE OBSTACLES CAN BE OVERCOME IN GLORY BY AN INDOMITABLE WILL AND PRE-VAILING FAITH.[17]

—comments from officials during Ben and Valerie Hogan Day in Fort Worth

BEN WAS THE GREATEST GOLFER YOU EVER DREAMED OF SEEING.[18]

—Tommy Bolt

I AM NOT ONE WHO BELIEVES MY ERA WAS THE GREATEST
NECESSARILY BECAUSE I LIVED IN IT. PEOPLE TODAY RUN
FASTER, JUMP HIGHER, AND RUN FARTHER, AND IT'S ONLY
NATURAL THAT THEY PLAY GOLF BETTER. BEN HAS PRETTY
WELL PROVED THAT THEY CAN. BUT THE THING THAT MAKES
A CHAMPION IS NOT NECESSARILY PRECISION PLAY. THE MAN
WHO WORKS THE HARDEST WINS THE CHAMPIONSHIPS. BEN,
WITH THE GAME HE HAS, WILL KEEP WINNING CHAMPI-
ONSHIPS AS LONG AS HE WANTS TO BADLY ENOUGH.[19]

—Bobby Jones at the dinner and celebration
following Hogan's return from the British Open

IF YOU CAN THINK OF BEN HOGAN AND NOT THINK OF GOLF,
OR THINK OF GOLF AND NOT BEN HOGAN, YOUR MIND IS
CAPABLE OF MAKING DISTINCTIONS THAT DO NOT EXIST. THE
RECORD, REMARKABLE AS IT IS, WAS NOT CREATED IN A VAC-
UUM. BEHIND THE RECORD STANDS A MAN OF UNDISCOUR-
AGEABLE AMBITION, OF DAUNTLESS COURAGE, OF RELENT-
LESS CONCENTRATION, OF KEEN INTELLIGENCE, OF AMAZING
INNER RESERVES . . .

—Granville T. Walker, family friend,
July 27, 1953, in a speech at a Ben Hogan luncheon

THE SPORT MAY NEVER SEE ANOTHER LIKE HIM.[20]

—Tim Finchem

⌒

I THINK PROBABLY SAM SNEAD WAS MORE NATURALLY TAL-
ENTED, BUT BEN HOGAN WAS UNMATCHED IN HIS DESIRE TO
BE THE BEST.[21]

—Pat Summerall, former golf commentator

⌒

HE WAS THE BEST WHO EVER PLAYED.[22]

—Lee Trevino, golfer

⌒

WELL, YOU'RE ASKING ME A QUESTION THAT'S EXTREMELY
DIFFICULT TO ANSWER. I'LL SAY THIS. I DON'T THINK THERE'S
EVER BEEN ANOTHER YEAR, WORLDWIDE, LIKE HIS [TIGER
WOODS'S]. EVER. DOES THAT ANSWER YOUR QUESTION?[23]

*—Byron Nelson, when asked if Ben Hogan, who won three
majors in 1953, ever had a year like Tiger Woods in 2000*

⌒

HOGAN'S VICTORY STAMPS HIM AS THE WORLD'S GREATEST GOLFER OF THIS, IF NOT ALL, TIMES.[24]

—Desmond Hackett, writer

BEN WOULD HAVE CONSIDERED TIGER A BETTER PLAYER THAN HIMSELF BECAUSE OF HIS LENGTH AND BECAUSE OF THE WAY HE READS GREENS. BEN WAS SO MUCH IN AWE OF LENGTH, HE'D HAVE BEEN IN AWE OF TIGER. HE WOULD HAVE SAID TIGER SHOULD WIN EVERY TOURNAMENT BECAUSE OF HIS LENGTH.[25]

—Dan Jenkins, when asked to compare Hogan and Tiger Woods

I WAS HITTING IT SO GOOD THAT DAY, HE STOPPED AND WATCHED ME. NOW THAT WAS INTIMIDATING.[26]

—Lanny Wadkins, recalling a time Hogan watched him practice

Well, then, you should be knocking the damn flagstick out of the holes.

—*Hogan's retort to Lanny Wadkins in the early nineties at Colonial when Wadkins made an innocent, off-the-cuff remark to Hogan about Colonial's browned-out fairways that year*

HE WAS THE GREATEST SHOTMAKER EVER. JACK NICKLAUS WAS THE GREATEST WINNER. BUT NOBODY HIT SHOTS LIKE HOGAN. THERE WAS AUTHORITY TO HIS SHOTS. AUTHORITY IS THE RIGHT WORD. THERE WAS A CRACK TO THEM.[27]

—*Dan Jenkins*

. . . THE BEST SHOTMAKER THE GAME HAS EVER SEEN.[28]

—*Jack Nicklaus*

NEW YORK IS ONLY A WAY STATION FOR THE PRECISIONIST OF THE FAIRWAYS, BUT THE CITY BOWS TO NONE IN APPRECIATION OF HIM, AS IT WILL AMPLY DEMONSTRATE. BY ADDING THE BRITISH OPEN CHAMPIONSHIP TO THE U.S. OPEN AND THE MASTERS, BEN HOGAN INCREASED HIS LUSTER AS A SPORTS IMMORTAL.[29]

—Lewis Burton, writer

MILLIONS OF AMERICANS WOULD LIKE TO PARTICIPATE WITH NEW YORKERS TODAY WHO ARE EXTENDING THEIR TRADITIONAL WELCOME ON YOUR RETURN FROM YOUR MAGNIFICENT VICTORY. WE ARE PROUD OF YOU, NOT ONLY AS A GREAT COMPETITOR AND AS A MASTER OF YOUR CRAFT, BUT ALSO AS AN ENVOY EXTRAORDINARY IN THE BUSINESS OF BUILDING FRIENDSHIP FOR AMERICA.

—excerpt from a telegram from President Eisenhower, read July 21, 1953

I've got a tough skin, but this kind of brings tears to my eyes. I don't think anything can surpass what's happening now.[30]

> *—Hogan during remarks at city hall following a ticker-tape parade in New York City following his victories in the Masters, U.S. Open, and British Open in 1953*

(JACK) NICKLAUS IS THE GREATEST PLAYER BECAUSE HE'S THE BEST PUTTER. BUT HOGAN WAS THE BEST SHOTMAKER. WHEN HE HIT THE BALL, IT LOOKED LIKE IT WAS FIRED OUT OF A RIFLE.[31]

> *—Claude Harmon*

I thanked them for the invitation, but I asked them to please put it off until I was dead.[32]

> *—Hogan's comment regarding his preference not to be honored at the Memorial Tournament*

This has been a wonderful day for me, the finest day I've ever had or ever will have—winning tournaments and all. I'd like to keep this day sort of sacred to us forever.[33]

> —Hogan's comment from a speech at the
> Worth Theater following the premier of Follow the Sun

Only in America could such a thing as this happen to a little guy like me.

> —excerpt from his comments at a ticker-tape parade in
> New York City honoring his three Grand Slam victories in 1953

I can't imagine people getting up so early to do this for us.[34]

> —discussing the celebration and
> ticker-tape parade in New York City

THE ONLY THING DIFFERENT ABOUT HOGAN'S PUTTING IS THAT HE'S GETTING HUMP-BACKED PICKING UP THOSE TEN-FOOT PUTTS OUT OF THE CAN.[35]

> —*Jimmy Demaret, talking about Hogan's new putting style*

THE GOLF COURSE IS WHAT DRIVES THE TRAIN AT OUR CLUB. BUT BEN HOGAN WAS THE ENGINEER WHO DROVE THE TRAIN AND PUT COLONIAL ON THE MAP. HIS WINS HERE BROUGHT A LOT OF HISTORY AND ATTENTION TO COLONIAL THAT WE PROBABLY WOULD NOT HAVE GOTTEN OTHERWISE.[36]

> —*Dr. Wally Schmuck, former Colonial Country Club president*

FRANKLY, WE WERE SURPRISED THAT HOGAN DIDN'T WIN EVERY TIME HE PLAYED.[37]

> —*Jerre Todd, former Colonial Invitation Tournament media room chairman*

ANYBODY THAT SHOOTS A 67 OUT THERE TODAY IS
A MIRACLE. I DON'T BELIEVE IT CAN BE DONE.[38]

> *—quote by an unidentified player, after Hogan*
> *shot a 67 in ninety-one-degree heat, with*
> *thirty-mile-per-hour winds, to win his fourth Colonial*

BEN HOGAN WON SO MANY TOURNAMENTS IT'S
SCARY. HE WAS INCREDIBLE. HE PLAYED AT A
LEVEL THAT NOT TOO MANY PLAYERS COULD
EVER ATTAIN.[39]

> *—Tiger Woods*

THE SECRET

> *Because Hogan came as close to perfecting the golf swing as any player who had ever played the game, many believed he had discovered a secret—the swing's most essential and critical element that he and he alone understood. In 1954, Life magazine offered him ten thousand dollars for a cover story about "the secret." Just before publication was scheduled, however, Hogan changed his mind and refused to agree to an interview.*

HE HAS IT UP HERE.[1]

> —Gene Sarazen, pointing to his head, in
> response to a question as to what Hogan's secret was

⌒

I won't even tell my wife.[2]

> —Hogan's comment while discussing
> his discovery of the secret of the golf swing

⌒

ANYBODY CAN SAY HE'S GOT A SECRET IF HE WON'T TELL WHAT IT IS.[3]

—*Sam Snead*

BEN HOGAN JUST KNOWS SOMETHING ABOUT HITTING A GOLF BALL THE REST OF US DON'T![4]

—*Mike Souchak, golfer*

BEFORE AND AFTER THE GLORY

Hogan wasn't always a great player. His first victory came a full nine years after he turned professional. And when he was at the end of his competitive career, unable to meet his own exacting standards, no one realized that sooner than Hogan himself. His playing career suffered an inglorious end: eleven over par after eleven holes during a round at the 1971 Houston Open. He signed his scorecard for the holes he had played, summoned a cart, and returned to the clubhouse, never again to play competitive golf.

I found out the first day I shouldn't even be there.[1]

—*Hogan's recollection of his first rounds as a professional, 78-75, at the 1930 Texas Open*

I REMEMBER SOME OF THE OLD-TIMERS TELLING ME THAT THEY USED TO SEE HIM OUT IN THERE IN THE THIRTIES, POUNDING AND HITTING BALLS AND TAKING BIG DIVOTS, AND THEY'D SAY, "WHO'S THAT KID OUT THERE? HE'S NOT GOING TO BE A PLAYER. WHY DOESN'T HE GO HOME?"[2]

—*Jack Fleck, golfer*

I never played in a $100,000 tournament in my life. I went broke twice . . . and had to take odd jobs to try again. It stops you when you can't eat or pay your caddie.[3]

—*Hogan discussing the difference on the PGA Tour when he played, and now*

Now you read about tournament winners getting $400,000. That's something. I was always looking forward to making the cut and winning last place, which was fifty dollars, so you could make enough gas money to get to the next one.[4]

—discussing the comparison of eras on the PGA Tour

It's no fun to hit balls because it hurts. Yes, I miss hitting balls. I love golf and swinging a golf club and hitting balls. That's been my life for a long time. I hated to give it up. I could hit chip shots around the green, but that's no fun.[5]

—remarking on his inability to play up to his expectations as he grew older

I'm through with competitive golf. From now on, I'm a weekend golfer.[6]

—Hogan's comment during the prize presentation after finishing second in a playoff for the 1955 U.S. Open

⌒

All the technique or practice in the world wasn't going to help me. It was a nerves situation, and it was embarrassing for me out there in front of people. I couldn't get the putter back.[7]

—his thoughts on when his putting started to desert him

⌒

I can't take a full swing now, just a short swing. I walk out there is about all I do.[8]

—recalling his decision to stop playing

⌒

It's a great disappointment not to come up to your level of expectations and the level necessary to compete.[9]

GOLFING WITH HOGAN

> *There was usually a story to tell when you were paired with Hogan.*

I SAW A MAGNIFICENT EXHIBITION OF HOW TO HIT A GOLF BALL.[1]

—*Jack Nicklaus, recalling the first time he played in a tournament with Hogan*

I just played with a kid who, if he had a brain in his head, would have won by ten shots.[2]

—*Hogan's comment recalling the first time he played with Jack Nicklaus, at the 1960 U.S. Open*

That's why they make eighteen holes.[3]

*—Hogan's response to fellow-competitor Ken Venturi,
who remarked to Hogan, "That's a hell of a way to start,"
after a double bogey at the first hole of a round*

You know, Claude, that's the first time I've ever birdied that hole.[4]

*—according to legend, Hogan's comment to Claude Harmon
after they played the par-three twelfth at Augusta National,
where Hogan made a birdie two and Harmon had a hole-in-one*

Ben with Valerie after he won the 1950 U.S. Open at Merion. *(United States Golf Association photo)*

THE MODERN GAME

> *Golf in the twenty-first century isn't the same game it was in Hogan's era, and it's obvious he didn't think it was necessarily for the better.*

They have better grasses, and the green superintendent knows how to take care of the grasses better and they have better chemicals. Everything is better nowadays, I don't care what it is. Whether you are talking about golf or baseball or hockey or automobiles, everything is better today. . . . It will be better tomorrow than it is today.[1]

The older ones, it seems to me, have done away with the backswing and the follow-through.[2]

  —*when asked what he thought of the Senior PGA Tour*

The players get paid. And the caddies get paid. . . . It is a strange thing, but I suppose the people who pay for it think they get their money's worth if it is shown on television. I never wore signs and I never will.[3]

  —*when asked about wearing corporate logos*

I don't watch that. It doesn't appeal to me. It isn't golf as I know it.[4]

  —*on the Skins Game concept*

The USGA wrote the rule; it ought to be enforced. You play by all of the rules anyway, don't you? They ought to enforce all the rules or don't have them. Or change the rule. One or the other.[5]

—on nonconforming equipment

To tell you where the pin is, I think that is a mistake. Using your judgment is part of golf. I used to play a golf course and I could tell you within four feet where every pin was going to be. I didn't know which day it would be there, but I knew it was going to be there. You can play a practice round on a golf course and tell where they are going to put the pin four days. We used to play a two-dollar Nassau on practice days and I never won one of them because I always shot where I thought the pin was going to be in the tournament. I never shot at the practice pin.[6]

—response to modern-day players'
over-reliance on exact yardages

ARCHITECTURE, AND OTHER GOLF COURSES

> *Hogan worked with renowned golf course architect Joe Lee on eighteen holes that now comprise the Hogan Course at the Trophy Club in suburban Dallas/Fort Worth. For many reasons the project failed to materialize as Hogan had envisioned, and that was his one and only involvement in golf course architecture.*

The terrain a lot of times has to do with what kind of golf course they can build on a piece of property. They have some awful good ones and some awful bad ones. Jeepers creepers, some of these things I see on television . . . [1]

Why build a torture chamber? Why not build something everybody can enjoy?[2]

⌒

You can get too much water on a golf course. I think almost every golf course needs a little water, on one or two or three holes, just for aesthetics. . . . But not too much. Not on damn near every hole.[3]

⌒

Almost every day there was a different angle with the wind. Normally it comes off the sea. That was a good training place for me late in the winter. The only thing I had to do from there when I went to Augusta was hit the ball higher.[4]

—*thoughts about Seminole in Juno Beach, Florida, his favorite course*

⌒

I like them tough, especially on the tee shot. Olympic, under U.S. Open conditions, puts a premium on every shot—the drive, the second shot, and the putt. Most courses don't do this. They let up on something. But there they don't. If you miss the fairway, you can't put the ball on the green from the rough.

I played with Jackie Burke in a practice round the first time I played out there. We had a little gallery, but he lost seven balls in eighteen holes. . . . The people in the gallery would say, "Well, it hit right there," and we would get down there and we couldn't find it. And Jackie was a good driver.[5]

—discussing the Olympic Club in
Daly City, California, his favorite U.S. Open site

The topography of the land may mean that sometimes you have to have a blind shot. But I don't like it. I can't play by radar.[6]

—discussing his aversion to blind shots

Hogan basically retired from competitive golf in the mid-fifties, but he came back every year to play a few tournaments, such as Colonial, the U.S. Open, and the Masters, until he was almost sixty. (United States Golf Association photo)

I have a lot of ideas on how a course should play, but I'm not an architect.[7]

HOGAN, THE CLUBMAKER

> Hogan was no less demanding of the clubs that bore his name. He once had $100,000 worth of new clubs discarded because they failed to meet his exacting standards.

We have a testing machine here—me.[1]

—joking about the test procedures
for the Hogan brand of clubs

I am just hardheaded enough and have faith enough in our profession to believe the plan will work.[2]

—when asked why he planned to
make a set of clubs named after him

If our experiment is successful, we'll be in the golf club-making business. If it's not, we won't.[3]

—discussing the possibility he might be interested in golf club manufacturing

He must be good. He uses Hogan clubs.

—in response to a question about Jack Fleck, who was still on the golf course, about to tie Hogan for the fourth-round lead at the 1955 U.S. Open

About a year or so after the Ben Hogan Company started operations, Hogan learned that his employees had been approached by a union organizer. At a workers' organizational meeting, Hogan spoke first, and this is what he said, according to Gardner Dickinson, who was on hand (from Curt Sampson's Hogan*):*

I understand that all of you fellows want to organize my business here and join a union. Well, that is certainly your privilege. If you'd like to pay a nice portion of your salaries to a union, be my guest. You obviously think that by organizing you're going to make a lot more money, and, in effect, tell me, the boss, what you're going to do. Before you vote, let me tell you just one thing: I've already started over once, and I can and will do so again, if necessary. So far, neither I nor my investors have made one damned cent. When we do make some money, I'll see to it that you make some, too. Until that happens, you're not going to make one more damned cent more than I can afford to pay you. And if any of you don't like those terms, you can go straight to the pay window and draw your severance pay, because in thirty minutes this plant will be operating full-blast again. Period.[4]

(The workers did not join the union.)

NOTES

Childhood:

1. *Fort Worth Star-Telegram*, July 27, 1997.
2. ESPN Classic, *50 Greatest Athletes of the 20th century*.
3. Ibid.
4. Ibid.
5. *Golf Digest*, October 1997.
6. Fort Worth *Business Press*, March 6, 1998.
7. ESPN Classic, *50 Greatest Athletes of the 20th century*.
8. *The Eternal Summer*, Curt Sampson. Taylor Publishing Company, Dallas, Texas, 1992, p. 28.

Practice and Preparation:

1. Told to Nick Seitz, *Golf Digest*.
2. *The Hogan Mystique*, article by Dave Anderson. The American Golfer, Greenwich, Conn., 1994, p. 15.
3. *Golf World*, August 1, 1997.
4. Associated Press, July 26, 1997.
5. *Fort Worth Star-Telegram*, May 1989 (exact date unknown).
6. Holidaycrafter.com.
7. *Fort Worth Star-Telegram*, July 12, 1999.
8. ESPN Classic, *50 Greatest Athletes of the 20th century*.
9. *Dallas Morning News*, May 8, 1994.
10. CBS, May 17, 1987.
11. ESPN Classic, *50 Greatest Athletes of the 20th Century*.
12. *The Hogan Mystique*, article by Ken Venturi, p. 68.
13. *The Hogan Mystique*, article by Ken Venturi, p. 127.
14. *Five Lessons: The Modern Fundamentals of Golf*, Ben Hogan, Simon and Schuster, New York, N.Y., 1957, p. 61.

15. *Dallas Morning News*, June 21, 1955.
16. *Five Lessons*, Hogan, p. 15.
17. *Dallas Morning News*, July 26, 1997.
18. *Five Lessons*, Hogan, p. 62.
19. CBS, May 17, 1987.
20. *Five Lessons*, Hogan, p. 14.
21. CBS, May 17, 1987.
22. Ibid.
23. *Golf Digest*, February 1998.
21. Ibid., p. 14.
23. CBS, May 17, 1987.
24. *Golf Digest*, February 1998.

A Man of Few Words:
1. Holland Sentinel Online Archives, posted June 9, 1999.
2. *The Hogan Mystique*, article by Dave Anderson, p. 19.
3. Associated Press, August 16, 2000.
4. *Dallas Morning News*, July 30, 1997.
5. CBS Radio, July 28, 1997.
6. *World News Tonight*, ABC, July 25, 1997.
7. *Time*, January 10, 1949.
8. *The Hogan Mystique*, article by Ken Venturi, p. 55.
9. *Hogan*, Curt Sampson. Rutledge Hill Press, Nashville, Tenn., 1996, p. xviii.

The Hogan Demeanor:
1. GolfJokes.co.uk.
2. *Fort Worth Star-Telegram*, May 1989 (exact date unknown).
3. Ibid.
4. Ibid.
5. Dan Perry's Links LS Web site.
6. *Golf Journal*, August 1997.
7. Ibid.
8. Ibid.

9. Ibid.
10. ESPN Classic, *50 Greatest Athletes of the 20th Century*.
11. *Golf World*, August 1, 1997.
12. *Golf Digest*, December 1994.
13. *Golf Digest*, October 1997.

The Game:
1. *Quotable Golfer*, Robert R. McCord. New York: The Lyons Press, 2000.
2. *Fort Worth Star-Telegram*, May 1989 (exact date unknown).
3. Associated Press, June 9, 1999.
4. *Fort Worth Star-Telegram*, June 15, 1953.
5. *Five Lessons*, Hogan, p. 126.
6. Ibid., p. 84.
7. *Hogan*, Sampson, p. 201.
8. *Fort Worth Star-Telegram*, July 11, 1953.
9. *Golf World*, August 1, 1997.
10. *Time*, January 10, 1949.
11. *Fort Worth Star-Telegram*, May 30, 1999.
12. *Financial Post*, Toronto, Ontario, Canada, July 30, 1997.
13. NBC Nightly News, July 25, 1997.
14. *Five Lessons*, Hogan, p. 15.
15. Ibid., p. 37.
16. Ibid., p. 97.
17. *The Eternal Summer*, Sampson, p. 31.
18. *Fort Worth Star-Telegram*, April 17, 1949.
19. *Las Vegas Review-Journal*, July 27, 1997.
20. *New York Times*, May 20, 1990.

The Swing:
1. *Fort Worth Star-Telegram*, May 1989 (exact date unknown).
2. Los Banos Sports.
3. "Famous Golf Quotes" Web site.

NOTES

4. Associated Press, July 28, 1997.

5. *The Hogan Mystique*, article by Ken Venturi, p. 88.

6. *Five Lessons*, Hogan, p. 14.

7. *Golf World*, August 1, 1997.

8. *Fort Worth Star-Telegram*, May 1989 (exact date unknown).

9. *Golf World*, April 14, 1948.

10. *Five Lessons*, Hogan, p. 57.

11. *USA Today*, July 28, 1997.

12. CBS, May 17, 1987.

13. *Time*, January 10, 1949.

14. CBS, May 17, 1987.

15. *USA Today*, July 15, 1991.

16. Los Banos Sports.

17. *Golf World*, August 1, 1997.

18. Ibid.

Characteristics of a Champion:

1. *USA Today*, July 15, 1991.

2. *Hogan*, Sampson, p. 83.

3. *Sports Illustrated*, August 4, 1997.

4. ESPN Classic, *50 Greatest Athletes of the 20th Century*.

5. Ibid.

6. Ibid.

7. Ibid.

8. *Pinehurst* (N.C.) *Outlook*, March 27, 1942.

9. *Dallas Morning News*, July 26, 1997.

10. World News Tonight, ABC, July 25, 1997.

11. ESPN Classic, *50 Greatest Athletes of the 20th Century*.

12. Ibid.

13. *San Antonio Express-News*, July 27, 1997.

14. *Fort Worth Star-Telegram*, July 27, 1997.

15. *Time*, January 10, 1949.

Notes

16. *Golf World*, August 1, 1997.
17. *Seattle Times*, July 29, 1997.
18. *Harvey Penick's Little Red Book: Lessons and Teachings from a Lifetime in Golf*, Harvey Penick with Bud Shrake.New York: Simon and Schuster, 1992, p. 151.
19. Ibid., p. 129.

The Hogan Reputation:
1. *The Hogan Mystique*, by Ben Crenshaw, p. 38.
2. CBS, May 17, 1987.
3. Ibid.
4. Jim Murray, *Los Angeles Times*, July 26, 1997.
5. *Dallas Morning News*, July 28, 1997.
6. *Seattle Post-Intelligencer*, July 29, 1997.
7. *Fort Worth Star-Telegram*, July 11, 1953.
8. *Fort Worth Star-Telegram*, May 25, 1953.
9. *Fort Worth Star-Telegram*, April 20, 1958.
10. ESPN Classic, *50 Greatest Athletes of the 20th Century*.
11. Australian Associated Press, July 29, 1997.
12. *Dallas Morning News*, July 26, 1997.

The Accident:
1. *Fort Worth Star-Telegram*, June 17, 1949.
2. *Fort Worth Star-Telegram*, April 29, 1949.
3. *Fort Worth Star-Telegram*, March 25, 1951.
4. ESPN Classic, *50 Greatest Athletes of the 20th Century*.
5. Ibid.
6. *Reader's Digest*, March 5, 1950.
7. *Golf World*, February 16, 1949.
8. Associated Press, July 30, 1997.
9. ESPN Classic, *50 Greatest Athletes of the 20th Century*.
10. Ibid.
11. *Fort Worth Star-Telegram*, March 25, 1951.
12. Ibid.

NOTES

The Comeback:

1. *Fort Worth Star-Telegram*, April 17, 1949.
2. *Fort Worth Star-Telegram*, June 16, 1949.
3. *Fort Worth Star-Telegram*, March 29, 1949.
4. *Hogan*, Sampson, p. 147.
5. ESPN Classic, *50 Greatest Athletes of the 20th Century*.
6. Ibid.
7. *Fort Worth Star-Telegram*, April 2, 1949.
8. *Fort Worth Star-Telegram*, January 11, 1950.
9. *Fort Worth Star-Telegram*, March 29, 1949.
10. *Fort Worth Star-Telegram*, April 17, 1949.
11. *Fort Worth Star-Telegram*, May 21, 1991.

Major Championships:

1. *Hogan*, Sampson, p. 147.
2. Ibid., p. 229.
3. *The U.S. Open, Golf's Ultimate Challenge*, Robert Sommers, Oxford University Press, New York, 1996, p. 140.
4. CBS-TV, May 17, 1987.
5. *Dallas Morning News*, July 12, 1999.
6. Associated Press, July 26, 1997.
7. *Fort Worth Star-Telegram*, June 14, 1953.
8. *Golf World*, April 17, 1953.
9. *Golf World*, June 22, 1951.
10. *Golf World*, August 17, 1951.
11. *Daily Sketch* newspaper, Scotland, July 11, 1953.
12. *Fort Worth Star-Telegram*, June 15, 1953.
13. *Fort Worth Star-Telegram*, July 12, 1999.
14. Ibid.
15. *Fort Worth Star-Telegram*, July 22, 1953.
16. *Fort Worth Star-Telegram*, July 21, 1953.
17. CBS, May 17, 1987.

Notes

Hogan's Humor:

1. *Golf Digest*, October 1997, p. 128.
2. *Fort Worth Star-Telegram*, March 25, 1951.
3. Associated Press, July 30, 1997.
4. "Famous Golf Quotes" Web site.
5. *As Hogan Said: The 389 Best Things Ever Said about How to Play Golf*, Randy Voorhees. New York: Simon and Schuster, 2000.
6. *The Hogan Mystique*, article by Ken Venturi, p. 128.
7. Information and text of letter provided by Tim Scott, former Hogan Company employee.
8. *Weekly Standard*, August 11, 1997.
9. *Fort Worth Star-Telegram*, July 21, 1953.

Tributes and Accolades:

1. ESPN Classic, *50 Greatest Athletes of the 20th Century*.
2. *Golf World*, April 23, 1954.
3. *Professional Golfer*, May 1954.
4. *Golf World*, April 13, 1951.
5. *Golf Journal*, August 1997.
6. *Golf World*, January 15, 1954.
7. CBS News, July 28, 1997.
8. *The Sporting News*, August 4, 1997.
9. *Fort Worth Star-Telegram*, July 11, 1953
10. *London Daily Telegraph*, July 11, 1953.
11. *Dallas Morning News*, July 28, 1997.
12. *New York Daily News*, August 14, 1997.
13. *Fort Worth Star-Telegram*, July 27, 1997.
14. *Dallas Morning News*, July 26, 1997.
15. CBS News, July 28, 1997.
16. *London Daily Express*, July 11, 1953.
17. *Fort Worth Star-Telegram*, July 28, 1953.
18. *The Sporting News*, August 4, 1997.
19. *Fort Worth Star-Telegram*, July 24, 1953.

20. Associated Press, July 30, 1997.

21. ESPN Classic, *50 Greatest Athletes of the 20th Century.*

22. Associated Press, July 26, 1997.

23. *Dallas Morning News*, August 23, 2000.

24. *London Daily Express*, July 11, 1953.

25. *Fort Worth Star-Telegram*, August 21, 2000.

26. *Golf Journal*, August 1997.

27. *Dallas Morning News*, July 30, 1997.

28. *Golf World*, August 1, 1997.

29. *New York Journal-American*, July 21, 1953.

30. *Hogan*, Sampson, p. 197.

31. *USA Today*, July 28, 1997.

32. *Hogan*, Sampson, p. 238.

33. *Golf World*, March 30, 1951.

34. *Fort Worth Star-Telegram*, July 21, 1953.

35. *Golf World*, February 2, 1949.

36. *Fort Worth Star-Telegram*, March 8, 2000.

37. *Fort Worth Star-Telegram*, Feb. 7, 2000.

38. *Fort Worth Star-Telegram*, May 25, 1953,

39. *Fort Worth Star-Telegram*, Aug. 21, 2000.

The Secret:

1. *Hogan*, Sampson, p. 201.

2. *Golf World*, January 12, 1949.

3. *Dallas Morning News*, May 15, 1996.

4. *Los Angeles Times*, July 26, 1997.

Before and After the Glory:

1. *Hogan*, Sampson, p. 39.

2. ESPN Classic, *50 Greatest Athletes of the 20th Century.*

3. Associated Press., July 30, 1997.

4. *Fort Worth Star-Telegram*, July 27, 1997.

5. *Dallas Morning News*, July 26, 1997.

Notes

6. *Hogan*, Sampson, p. 217.

7. CBS, May 17, 1987.

8. *Dallas Morning News*, July 26, 1997.

9. *USA Today*, July 15, 1991.

Golfing with Hogan:

1. ESPN Classic, *50 Greatest Athletes of the 20th Century*.

2. *Golf Journal*, August 1997.

3. *Golf World*, August 1, 1997.

4. *Dallas Morning News*, July 26, 1997.

The Modern Game:

1. CBS, May 17, 1987.

2. Ibid.

3. Ibid.

4. Ibid.

5. Ibid.

6. Ibid.

Architecture, and Other Courses:

1. CBS, May 17, 1987.

2. Ibid.

3. Ibid.

4. Ibid.

5. Ibid.

6. Ibid.

7. *Golf Digest*, December 1997.

Hogan, the Clubmaker:

1. *Fort Worth Star-Telegram*, October 25, 1999.

2. *Professional Golfer*, May 1954.

3. *Fort Worth Star-Telegram*, July 25, 1953.

4. *Hogan*, Sampson, pp. 206–07.